PIANO · VOCAL · GUITAR

COUNTRY SHEET MUSIC

⟫⟫⟫ 2010–2019 ⟪⟪⟪

ISBN 978-1-5400-9175-8

HAL•LEONARD®

Visit Hal Leonard Online at
www.halleonard.com

Contact us:
Hal Leonard
7777 West Bluemound Road
Milwaukee, WI 53213
Email: info@halleonard.com

In Europe, contact:
Hal Leonard Europe Limited
42 Wigmore Street
Marylebone, London, W1U 2RN
Email: info@halleonardeurope.com

In Australia, contact:
Hal Leonard Australia Pty. Ltd.
4 Lentara Court
Cheltenham, Victoria, 3192 Australia
Email: info@halleonard.com.au

CONTENTS

AMERICAN HONEY

Words and Music by HILLARY LINDSEY,
SHANE STEVENS and CARY BARLOWE

She grew _

up _____ on the side of the road _____ where the church bells _

* Recorded a half step lower.

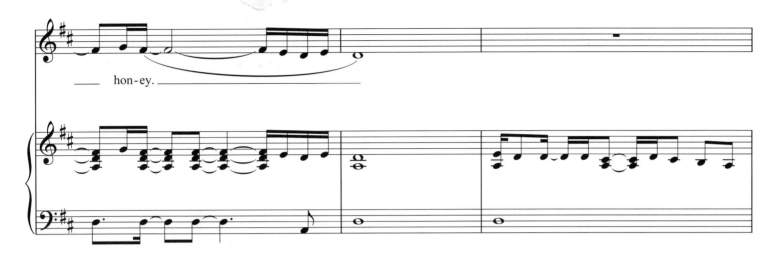

hon-ey.

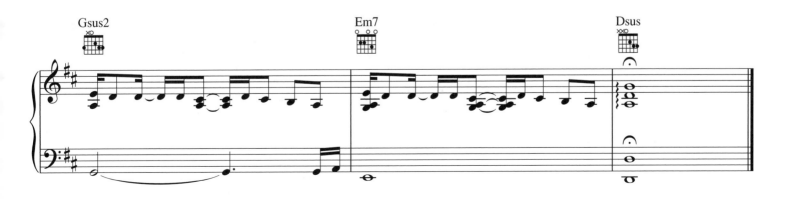

BISCUITS

Words and Music by KACEY MUSGRAVES,
SHANE McANALLY and BRANDY CLARK

Taking down your neighbor won't take you any higher.

I burned my own damn finger poking

No - bod - y's per -

- fect; __ we've all lost, and we've all lied.

BLUE AIN'T YOUR COLOR

Words and Music by HILLARY LINDSEY,
STEVEN LEE OLSEN and CLINT LAGERBERG

I can see you o-ver there, star-ing at your drink, watch-ing that ice sink all a-

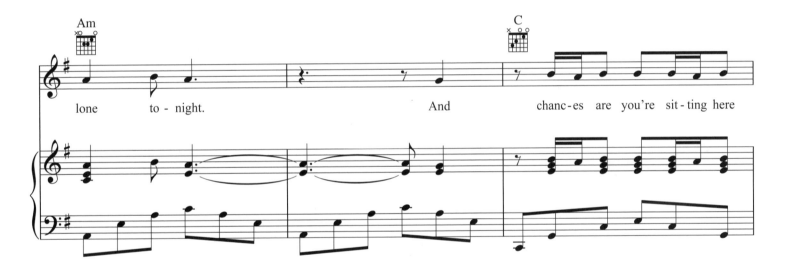

lone to-night. And chanc-es are you're sit-ting here

in this bar__ 'cause he ain't gon-na treat you right.__ Well, it's__

be an-oth-er "just pick you up" kind of guy tryin' to drink you up, __ tryin' __ to take you home.

But I just don't un-der-stand how an-oth-er man can take your sun and turn

it ice cold. __ Well, I've __ had e-nough to drink, and it's

mak-ing me think __ that I _____ just might ____ tell you: __

BODY LIKE A BACK ROAD

Words and Music by SAM HUNT,
JOSH OSBORNE, SHANE McANALLY
and ZACH CROWELL

BREAK UP WITH HIM

Words and Music by BRAD TURSI,
TREVOR ROSEN, MATT RAMSEY,
GEORGE SPRUNG and WILLIAM SELLERS

(Spoken:) Hey, girl, what's up?

(Spoken:) I know you don't wanna break his heart. But that ain't no good rea-son to be keep-in' us a-part. Look,

I know it's late, but I knew you'd pick it up.

up with him. The way ___ you look at me, girl, you can't pre-tend. I

know you ain't in love with him. Break up with him.

(Spoken:) Just break up with him.

BROKEN HALOS

Words and Music by CHRIS STAPLETON
and MIKE HENDERSON

BURNING HOUSE

Words and Music by JEFF BHASKER,
TYLER SAM JOHNSON and CAMARON OCHS

Moderately fast

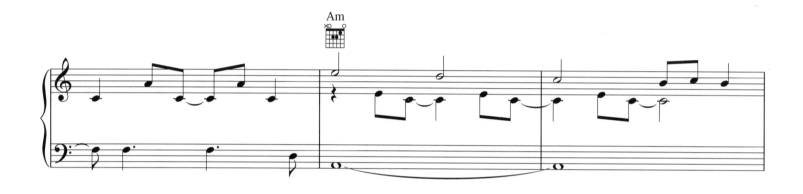

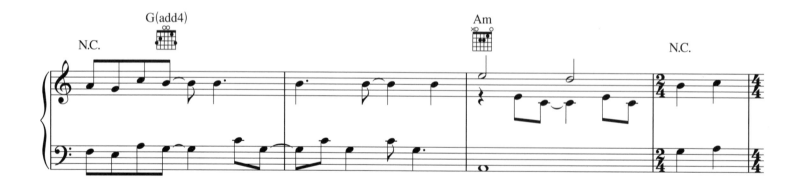

CRAZY GIRL

Words and Music by LIZ ROSE
and LEE BRICE

I told you late - ly I love you like cra -

- zy, girl? _____

cra - zy, girl? _____

Like

cra - zy, girl.

Like cra - zy, _____ like

cra - zy, girl. _____

CROWDED TABLE

Words and Music by NATALIE HEMBY,
LORI McKENNA and BRANDI CARLILE

Recorded a half step lower.

CRUISE

Words and Music by CHASE RICE,
TYLER HUBBARD, BRIAN KELLEY,
JOEY MOI and JESSE RICE

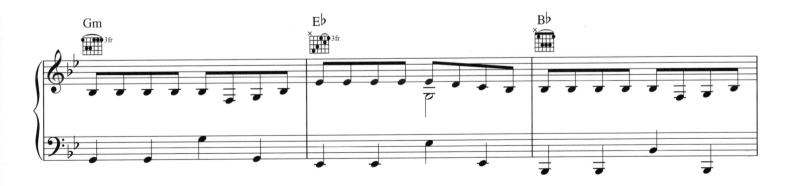

DIRT ROAD ANTHEM

Words and Music by BRANTLEY GILBERT
and COLT FORD

DRINK ON IT

Words and Music by JESSI ALEXANDER,
JON RANDALL and RODNEY CLAWSON

D.S. al Coda

DRINKIN' PROBLEM

Words and Music by JESS CARSON,
MARK WYSTRACH, CAMERON DUDDY,
SHANE McANALLY and JOSH OSBORNE

HEARTACHE MEDICATION

Words and Music by JON PARDI,
NATALIE HEMBY and BARRY DEAN

Moderate Country, in 2

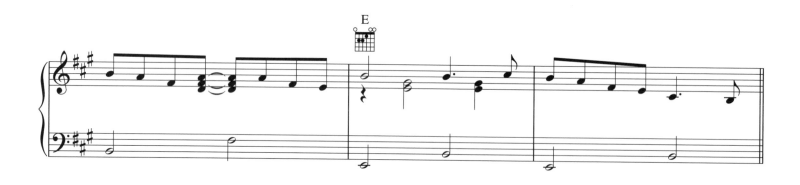

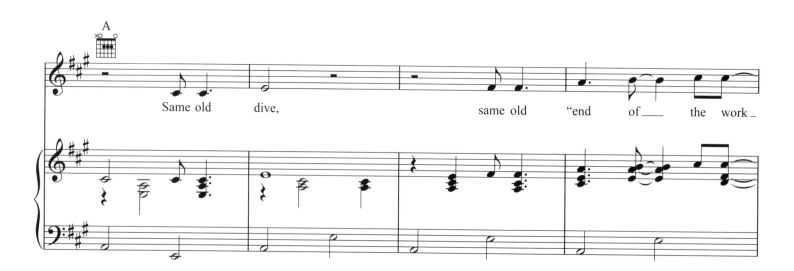

Same old dive, same old "end of ___ the work ___

o - ver ___ you. ___ Turn - in' me ___ loose ___ on ___ that

hard - wood ___ juke - box, lost in ne - on ___ time. ___ My

heart - ache med - i - ca - tion, well, it suits me ___ fine. ___ And I'm

drink - in' e - nough ___ to take you off ___ my mind.

Steel guitar solo ad lib.

To Coda

I'll prob-'ly find me some trou-ble.

D.S. al Coda

N.C.

And

CODA

A

mind.
(Lead vocal ad lib. on repeats)

I got my heart-ache med-i-ca-tion.

Bm

E

A

Play 3 times

HOMESICK

Words and Music by KANE BROWN,
MATTHEW McGINN, BROCK BERRYHILL
and TAYLOR PHILLIPS

lone __ with __ your brown eyes, all tan-gled up, just hold - ing __

on to you to-night un-til __ morn - ing. __ Ba-by, that's the damn __ truth. __ If

To Coda ⊕

home is where __ the heart __ is, I'm home - sick __ for you. __

Well, it says __ "Kane Brown" __ on a sign, with a line out the door. __

HUMBLE AND KIND

Words and Music by
LORI McKENNA

Moderately, with a lilt

You know there's a light ___ that glows ___ by the front ___
pect a free ride ___ from no ___

* Recorded a half step higher.

I DON'T DANCE

Words and Music by LEE BRICE,
DALLAS DAVIDSON and ROB HATCH

* *Recorded a half step higher.*

IF I DIE YOUNG

Words and Music by
KIMBERLY PERRY

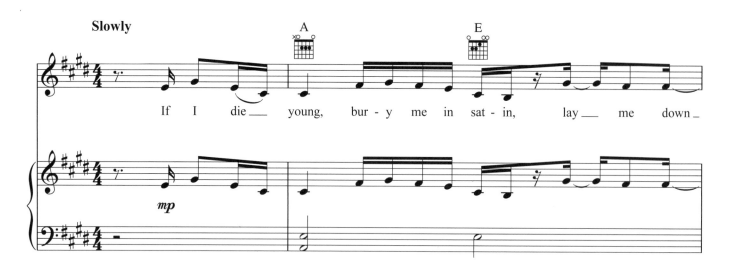

If I die___ young, bur-y me in sat-in, lay___ me down___

___ on a bed of ros-es. Sink___ me in the riv-er at dawn,___ send___ me a-

way ___ with the words of a love song. Uh oh,___ uh oh.___ Lord, make me a

MEAN

Words and Music by
TAYLOR SWIFT

Moderately fast

MARRY ME

Words and Music by THOMAS RHETT,
SHANE McANALLY, ASHLEY GORLEY
and JESSE FRASURE

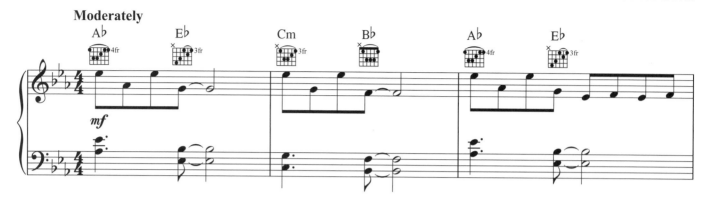

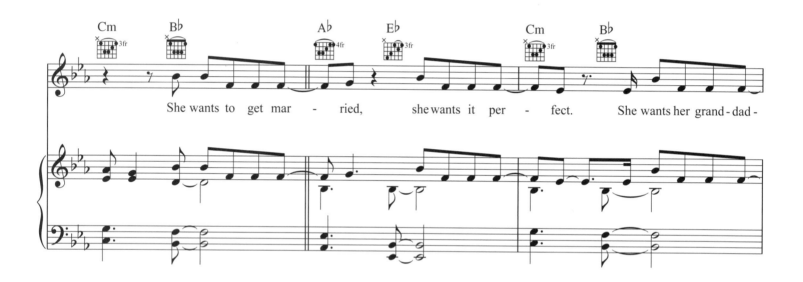

bod - y sees.___ Yeah, she wan - na get mar - ried, ___

To Coda ⊕

but she don't wan - na mar - ry me.

I re-mem-ber the night ___ when I al-most kissed ___ her. Yeah, I kind-a freaked ___

___ out. We'd been friends for for - ev - er. And I'd al - ways won -

PONTOON

Words and Music by BARRY DEAN,
LUKE LAIRD and NATALIE HEMBY

pon - toon,   ooh ooh ooh. ___

On the pon - toon,   ooh ooh ooh.

Back this hitch out in - to the wa - ter.   On the pon - toon,

ooh ooh ooh. ___   Ooh ooh ooh. ___

MERCY

Words and Music by SEAN McCONNELL
and BRETT YOUNG

MOST PEOPLE ARE GOOD

Words and Music by JOSH KEAR,
DAVID FRASIER and EDWARD MONROE HILL

I be - lieve __ that days ___ go slow and years __

__ go fast. And ev - 'ry breath's __ a gift, __

MY CHURCH

Words and Music by busbee
and MAREN MORRIS

THE ONE THAT GOT AWAY

Words and Music by JOSHUA OWEN,
DALLAS DAVIDSON and JIMMY RITCHEY

She rolled in my lit-tle sand-y town.
kissed my lips down on O-cean Drive.

She spent the
She set my

RIDIN' ROADS

Words and Music by ZACH CROWELL,
DUSTIN LYNCH and ASHLEY GORLEY

SPRINGSTEEN

Words and Music by ERIC CHURCH,
JEFFERY HYDE and RYAN TYNDELL

To this day____ when I hear that song,____ I see you stand - in' there on that lawn,____ dis-count shades,____ store-bought tan,____ flip flops and cut - off jeans.____ Some-where be-tween that set - tin' sun,____

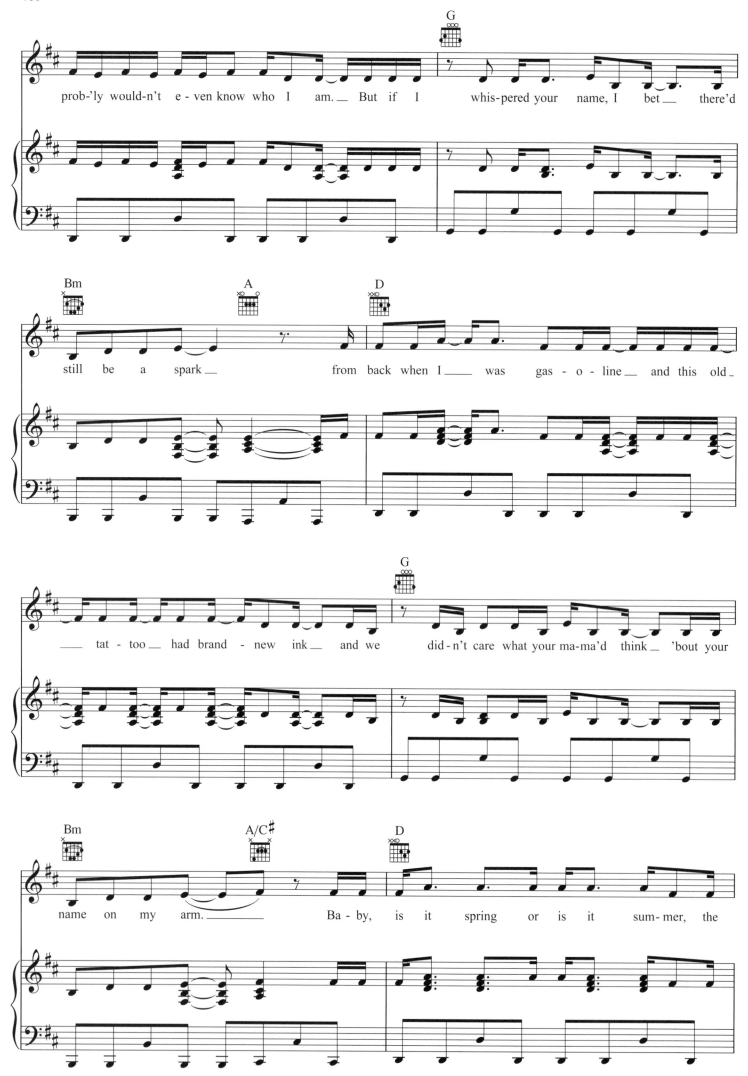

SOMETHING IN THE WATER

Words and Music by CHRIS DESTEFANO,
CARRIE UNDERWOOD and BRETT JAMES

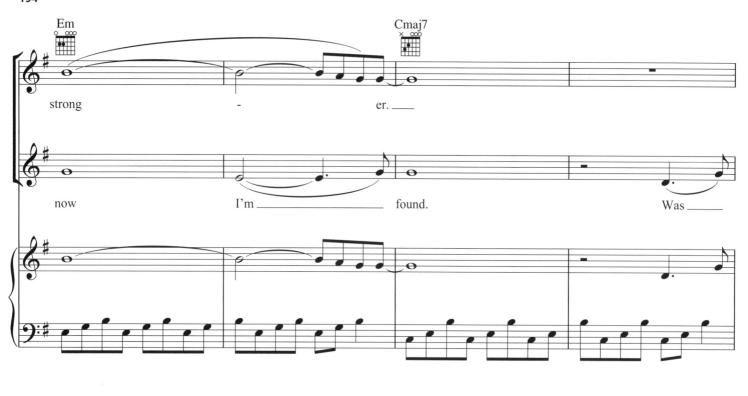

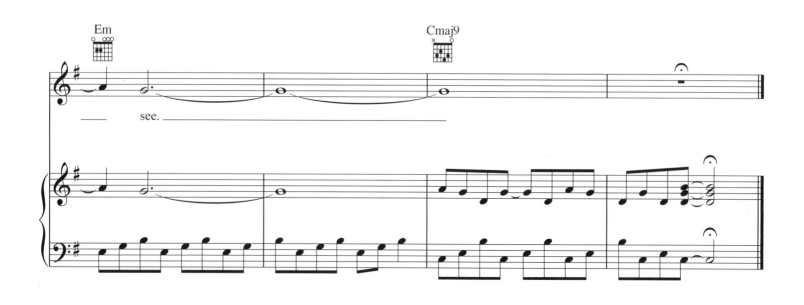

STUCK LIKE GLUE

Words and Music by KRISTIAN BUSH,
SHY CARTER, Kevin Griffin
and JENNIFER NETTLES

Recorded a half step lower.

TEQUILA

Words and Music by DAN SMYERS,
JORDAN REYNOLDS and NICOLLE GALYON

* Recorded a half step lower.

THIS IS IT

Words and Music by SCOTTY McCREERY,
FRANK ROGERS and AARON ESHUIS

WHEN IT RAINS IT POURS

Words and Music by LUKE COMBS,
RAY FULCHER and JORDAN WALKER

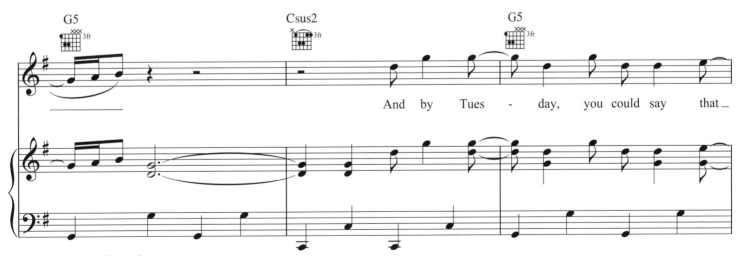

Recorded a half step lower.

TIL MY LAST DAY

Words and Music by JEREMY STOVER,
BRIAN MAHER and JUSTIN MOORE

Peo-ple say I'm just _____ a rough _____
Ba-by, I might _____ meet all _____

_____ boy, _____ I ain't no good for _____ you, girl. _____ It's a
_____ my _ friends, shoot the bull, have a beer or two. _____ But _

TIN MAN

Words and Music by JON RANDALL,
JACK INGRAM and MIRANDA LAMBERT

Hey there, Mis-ter Tin ___ Man,
___ Man,
___ Man,

you don't know ___ how luck - y you are. ___
you don't know ___ how luck - y you are. ___
I'm glad ___ we talked ___ this ___ out. ___

WANTED

Words and Music by HUNTER HAYES
and TROY VERGES

WHY DON'T WE JUST DANCE

Words and Music by JIM BEAVERS,
JONATHAN SINGLETON and DARRELL BROWN

Oh, __ ba - by,

why don't we just dance? __

YEAH BOY

Words and Music by KELSEA BALLERINI,
FOREST GLEN WHITEHEAD and KEESY TIMMER

YOU SHOULD BE HERE

Words and Music by COLE SWINDELL
and ASHLEY GORLEY

YOU AND TEQUILA

Words and Music by MATRACA BERG
and DEANA CARTER

* Recorded a half step lower.

YOURS

Words and Music by RUSSELL DICKERSON,
CASEY BROWN and PARKER WELLING

Country Pop beat, in 2

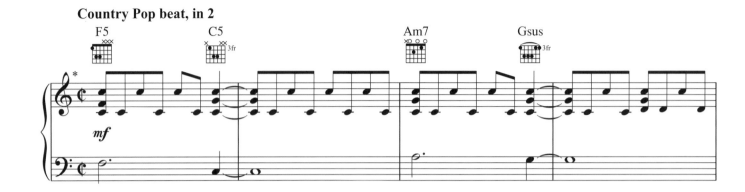

I was a
boat stuck in a bot-tle that nev-er got the chance to touch __ the sea; just for-

* *Recorded a half step lower.*